Songs from Mother Goose

Songs
from
Mother Goose
With the Traditional Melody for Each

Compiled by Nancy Larrick
Illustrated by Robin Spowart

Harper & Row, Publishers

Songs from Mother Goose: With the Traditional Melody for Each

Typography by Connie Fogler
1 2 3 4 5 6 7 8 9 10
First Edition

Library of Congress Cataloging-in-Publication Data
Songs from Mother Goose.

Includes index.
Summary: A collection of Mother Goose rhymes including
music, illustrations, an introduction by the compiler,
and a selection of historical notes.
1. Children's songs.   2. Nursery rhymes—Musical
settings.   [1. Nursery rhymes.   2. Songs]   I. Larrick,
Nancy.   II. Spowart, Robin, ill.
M1997.S6898   1989   88-754466
ISBN 0-06-023713-9
ISBN 0-06-023714-7 (lib. bdg.)

Acknowledgments

For the musical notations in this book, I would like to express my appreciation to Lloyd Robb and Renée Cafiero, who worked on the adaptations of centuries-old tunes for young children to sing easily.

For advice and encouragement on the musical side of this project, I am grateful to Dr. Charlotte Collins of the Shenandoah Conservatory of Music.

And for invaluable guidance and inspiration, I am indebted to the work of Iona and Peter Opie, especially their *Oxford Dictionary of Nursery Rhymes*, first published in 1951.

Nancy Larrick

Contents

Introduction

Singing seems to bring a feeling of enchantment to children. The infant is soothed by the soft crooning voice of mother or father. Older children skip or dance as the rhythm suggests and chime in on repeated lines. At school and on the playground, games that involve singing draw groups together easily and happily.

Some of the best-loved songs for children are those we associate with Mother Goose. You may have heard the words of a nursery rhyme and not have known that there is also a melody. Or you may have learned the words and melody of a favorite camp song and not associated it with Mother Goose. But the magic is there nonetheless.

For hundreds of years children of the English-speaking world have been entertained by the lullabies, singing games, verse stories, and nonsense jingles that we call the nursery rhymes of Mother Goose. They seem to have everything that appeals to children.

Even a baby is caught up by the musical quality and variation, swinging and swaying to the lilting rhythm of "Dance to Your Daddy." A little later the same child will be ready for a good "gallop" on your knee to the beat of "Ride a Cock-Horse."

Children relish the nonsense of "Hey Diddle Diddle" and "There Was a Lady Loved a Swine." They are quick to chime in on such sound-effect words as "Hickety, pickety" and "Cock-a-doodle doo!" They chuckle over the little drama of "Six Little Mice Sat Down to Spin" or "Jack and Jill."

Animals, birds, children, kings, lovers, simpletons, street vendors—all are here in the Mother Goose rhymes. Some of the rhymes are humorous, some joyous, some tender, even sad. All cry out to be sung and listened to. Each one invites the child to become involved through singing, clapping, dancing, feeling.

Many children's songbooks are designed for the piano rack, thus putting words and pictures beyond the immediate reach and involvement of the young child while he or she listens.

Sing a Song of Mother Goose is designed as a lap book, to be spread out before adult and child. The musical notations are simple enough for even the nonmusical person to follow. As the adult sings words and melody, the child can enjoy the related picture and soon will be singing repeated words and phrases. Then it's time for talk about the song and the picture.

Then "Let's sing it again!" and the fun starts all over.

As you sing these Mother Goose songs with children, I think you will find them reaching out happily to respond and create on their own. Next time, they'll say, "Let's sing a song of Mother Goose!"

—Nancy Larrick

Hickory, Dickory, Dock

Hickory, Dickory, Dock

Hickory, dickory, dock,
The mouse ran up the clock.
   The clock struck one,
   The mouse ran down,
Hickory, dickory, dock.

Hick-o - ry, dick-o - ry,   dock, __ The

mouse ran up   the   clock. __ The

clock struck one,   The   mouse ran down,

Hick - o - ry, dick - o - ry,   dock.

Three Blind Mice

Three blind mice, see how they run!
They all ran after the farmer's wife,
Who cut off their tails with a carving knife,
Did you ever see such a thing in your life,
   As three blind mice?

Three blind   mice,   see   how   they

run!   They   all ran af-ter the   farm-er's wife,

Who   cut off their tails with a   carv-ing knife,

Did   you ev-er see such a   thing in your life,

As   three   blind   mice? __

Six Little Mice Sat Down to Spin

Six little mice sat down to spin;
Pussy passed by and she peeped in.
What are you doing, my little men?
Weaving coats for gentlemen.
Shall I come in and cut off your threads?
Oh, no, Mistress Pussy, you'd bite off our heads.

Six lit-tle mice sat down to spin;

Pus-sy passed by and she peeped in.

What are you do-ing, my lit-tle men?

Weav-ing coats for gen-tle-men.

Shall I come in and cut off your threads? Oh,

no, Mis-tress Pus-sy, you'd bite off our heads.

Three Little Kittens

Three little kittens they lost their mittens,
   And they began to cry,
Oh, mother dear, we sadly fear
   That we have lost our mittens.
What! lost your mittens, you naughty kittens!
   Then you shall have no pie.
   Mee-ow, mee-ow.
   Then you shall have no pie.

Three little kittens they found their mittens,
   And they began to cry,
Oh, mother dear, see here, see here,
   For we have found our mittens.
Put on your mittens, you silly kittens,
   And you shall have some pie.
   Purr-r, purr-r.
   Oh, let us have some pie.

Three little kittens put on their mittens,
    And soon ate up the pie;
Oh, mother dear, we greatly fear
    That we have soiled our mittens.
What! soiled your mittens, you naughty kittens!
    Then they began to sigh.
    Mee-ow, mee-ow.
    Then they began to sigh.

Three little kittens they washed their mittens,
    And hung them out to dry;
Oh, mother dear, do you not hear
    That we have washed our mittens?
What! washed your mittens, then you're good kittens,
    But I smell a rat close by.
    Mee-ow, mee-ow.
    We smell a rat close by.

5

Pussy Cat, Pussy Cat

Pussy cat, pussy cat, where have you been?
I've been to London to look at the queen.
Pussy cat, pussy cat, what did you there?
Frightened a little mouse under her chair.

Pus-sy cat, pus-sy cat, where have you been?

I've been to Lon-don to look at the queen.

Pus-sy cat, pus-sy cat, what did you there?

Fright-ened a lit-tle mouse un-der her chair.

I Love Little Pussy

I love little pussy,
    Her coat is so warm,
And if I don't hurt her
    She'll do me no harm.
So I'll not pull her tail,
    Nor drive her away,
But pussy and I
    Very gently will play.

I love lit-tle pus-sy, Her coat is so warm, And

if I don't hurt her She'll do me no harm. So I'll

not pull her tail, Nor drive her a-way, But

pus-sy and I Ve-ry gent-ly will play.

Baa, Baa, Black Sheep

Baa, baa, black sheep,
  Have you any wool?
Yes, sir, yes, sir,
  Three bags full;
One for the master,
  And one for the dame,
And one for the little boy
  Who lives down the lane.

Baa, baa, black sheep, Have you an-y wool?

Yes, sir, yes, sir, Three bags full;

One for the mas-ter, And one for the dame, And

one for the lit-tle boy Who lives down the lane.

Hickety, Pickety, My Black Hen

Hickety, pickety, my black hen,
She lays eggs for gentlemen;
Sometimes nine and sometimes ten,
Hickety, pickety, my black hen.

Hick-e - ty, pick-e - ty,   my black hen,

She lays eggs   for   gen - tle-men;

Some-times nine   and   some-times ten,

Hick-e - ty, pick-e - ty,   my black hen.

8

Oh Where, Oh Where Has My Little Dog Gone?

Oh where, oh where has my little dog gone?
    Oh where, oh where can he be?
With his ears cut short and his tail cut long,
    Oh where, oh where is he?

Oh where, oh where has my lit-tle dog gone? Oh where, oh where can he be? With his ears cut short and his tail cut long, Oh where, oh where is he?

The North Wind Doth Blow

The north wind doth blow,
And we shall have snow,
And what will poor robin do then?
 Poor thing!
He'll sit in a barn,
And keep himself warm,
And hide his head under his wing.
 Poor thing!

The north wind doth blow, And we shall have

snow, And what will poor rob - in do

then? Poor thing! He'll sit in a

barn, And keep him - self warm, And

hide his head un - der his wing. Poor thing!

Boys and Girls Come Out to Play

Boys and Girls Come Out to Play

Boys and girls come out to play,

The moon doth shine as bright as day.

Leave your supper and leave your sleep,

And join your playfellows in the street.

Come with a whoop and come with a call,

Come with a good will or not at all.

Up the ladder and down the wall,

A halfpenny loaf will serve us all;

You find milk, and I'll find flour,

And we'll have a pudding in half an hour.

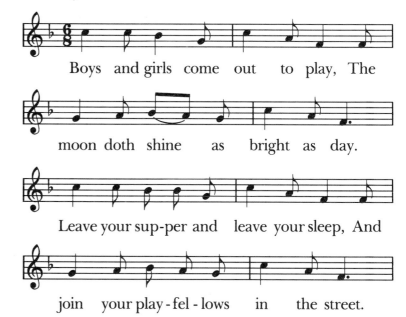

Boys and girls come out to play, The
moon doth shine as bright as day.
Leave your sup-per and leave your sleep, And
join your play-fel-lows in the street.

Georgie Porgie

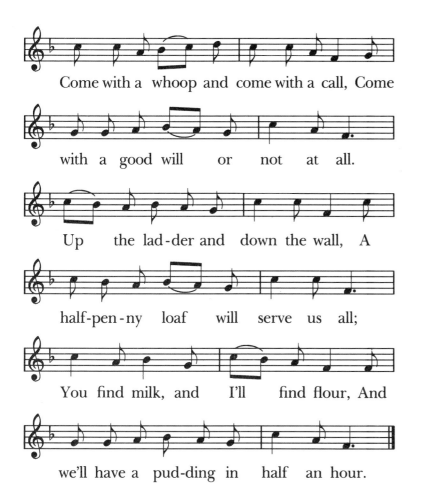

Come with a whoop and come with a call, Come

with a good will or not at all.

Up the lad-der and down the wall, A

half-pen-ny loaf will serve us all;

You find milk, and I'll find flour, And

we'll have a pud-ding in half an hour.

Georgie Porgie, pudding and pie,
Kissed the girls and made them cry;
When the boys came out to play,
Georgie Porgie ran away.

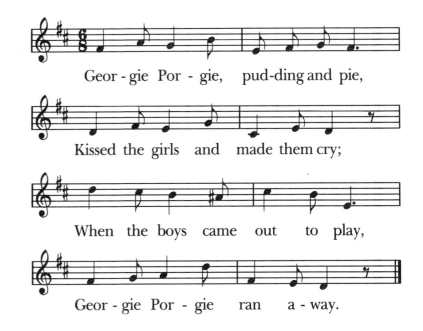

Geor - gie Por - gie, pud-ding and pie,

Kissed the girls and made them cry;

When the boys came out to play,

Geor - gie Por - gie ran a - way.

Jack and Jill

Jack and Jill went up the hill
  To fetch a pail of water;
Jack fell down and broke his crown,
  And Jill came tumbling after.

Up Jack got and home did trot,
  As fast as he could caper,
To old Dame Dob, who patched his nob
  With vinegar and brown paper.

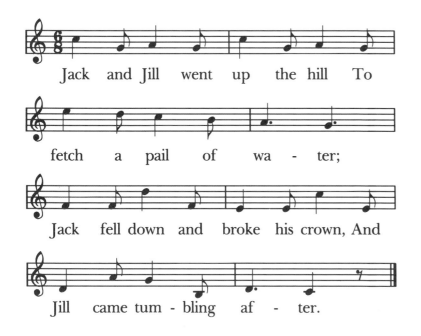

Jack and Jill went up the hill To
fetch a pail of wa - ter;
Jack fell down and broke his crown, And
Jill came tum - bling af - ter.

Little Boy Blue

Little Boy Blue,
　Come blow your horn,
The sheep's in the meadow,
　The cow's in the corn;
But where's the boy
　Who looks after the sheep?
He's under a haycock,
　Fast asleep.
Will you wake him?
　No, not I!
For if I do,
　He's sure to cry.

Lit - tle Boy Blue, Come blow your horn,

The sheep's in the mead-ow, The cow's in the corn;

But where's the boy Who looks af - ter the sheep?

He's un - der a hay - cock Fast a - sleep.

Will you wake him? No, not I! For

if I do, He's sure to cry.

Little Bo-peep

Lit-tle Bo-peep has lost her sheep, And

can't tell where to find them;

Leave them a-lone, and they'll come home, And

bring their tails be - hind them.

Little Bo-peep has lost her sheep,
  And can't tell where to find them;
Leave them alone, and they'll come home,
  And bring their tails behind them.

Little Bo-peep fell fast asleep,
  And dreamed she heard them bleating;
And when she awoke, she found it a joke,
  For they were still all fleeting.

Then up she took her little crook,
  Determined for to find them;
She found them indeed, but it made her heart bleed,
  For they'd left their tails behind them.

It happened one day, as Bo-peep did stray
  Into a meadow hard by,
There she espied their tails side by side,
  All hung on a tree to dry.

She heaved a sigh, and wiped her eye,
  And over the hillocks went rambling,
And tried what she could, as a shepherdess should,
  To tack again each to its lambkin.

Little Tommy Tucker

Little Tommy Tucker
  Sings for his supper:
What shall we give him?
  White bread and butter.
How shall he cut it
  Without a knife?
How will he be married
  Without a wife?

Lit-tle Tom-my Tuck-er   Sings   for his

sup - per: What shall we give him?

White bread and but - ter.   How shall he

cut   it With - out   a   knife?

How will he be mar-ried With-out a wife?

17

Little Jack Horner

Little Jack Horner
Sat in the corner,
Eating a Christmas pie;
He put in his thumb,
And pulled out a plum,
And said, What a good boy am I!

Lit-tle Jack Hor-ner   Sat in the cor-ner,

Eat-ing   a   Christ-mas   pie; _____   He

put in his thumb, And pulled out a plum, And

said, What a good boy am   I! _____

Little Miss Muffet

Little Miss Muffet,
She sat on a tuffet,
Eating her curds and whey;
Along came a spider,
Who sat down beside her
And frightened Miss Muffet away.

Lit-tle Miss Muf-fet, She sat on a tuf-fet,

Eat-ing her curds   and   whey; __   A -

long came a spi-der Who   sat down be-side her

And fright-ened Miss Muf-fet a - way. __

Lucy Locket

Lucy Locket lost her pocket,
Kitty Fisher found it;
Not a penny was there in it,
Only ribbon round it.

Lu - cy Lock - et   lost her pock - et,

Kit - ty Fish - er   found   it;

Not   a   pen - ny   was there in   it,

On - ly   rib - bon   round   it.

Mary Had a Little Lamb

Mary had a little lamb,
    Little lamb, little lamb,
Mary had a little lamb,
    Its fleece was white as snow.

And everywhere that Mary went,
    Mary went, Mary went,
Everywhere that Mary went,
    The lamb was sure to go.

It followed her to school one day,
    School one day, school one day,
It followed her to school one day.
    That was against the rule.

It made the children laugh and play,
    Laugh and play, laugh and play,
It made the children laugh and play
    To see a lamb at school.

Mary, Mary, Quite Contrary

Mary, Mary, quite contrary,
How does your garden grow?
With silver bells and cockle shells,
And pretty maids all in a row.

Mar - y, Mar - y, quite con - trar - y,

How does your gar - den grow? With

sil - ver bells and cock - le shells, And

pret - ty maids all in a row.

Polly Put the Kettle On

Polly put the kettle on,
Polly put the kettle on,
Polly put the kettle on,
   We'll all have tea.

Sukey take it off again,
Sukey take it off again,
Sukey take it off again,
   They've all gone away.

Tom, Tom, the Piper's Son

Tom, Tom, the piper's son,
Stole a pig and away he run;
    The pig was eat
    And Tom was beat,
And Tom went howling down the street.

Tom, Tom, the pi - per's son,

Stole a pig and a - way he run; The

pig was eat And Tom was beat, And

Tom went howl-ing down the street.

Tom, He Was a Piper's Son

Tom, he was a piper's son,
He learned to play when he was young,
But all the tune that he could play
Was "Over the Hills and Far Away."
Over the hills and a great way off,
The wind shall blow my topknot off.

Tom with his pipe made such a noise,
That he pleased both the girls and boys,
And they all stopped to hear him play
"Over the Hills and Far Away."
Over the hills and a great way off,
The wind shall blow my topknot off.

Tom, he was a pi-per's son, He

learned to play when he was young, But

all the tune that he could play Was

"O - ver the Hills and Far A - way."

O - ver the hills and a great way off, The

wind shall blow my top - knot off.

Ride a Cock-Horse

Ride a Cock-Horse to Banbury Cross

Ride a cock-horse to Banbury Cross,
To see a fine lady upon a white horse;
Rings on her fingers and bells on her toes,
She shall have music wherever she goes.

Ride a cock-horse to Ban-bur-y Cross, To

see a fine la-dy up - on a white horse;

Rings on her fin-gers and bells on her toes,

She shall have mu-sic wher - ev - er she goes.

How Many Miles to Babylon?

How many miles to Babylon?
    Three score and ten.
Can I get there by candlelight?
    Yes, and back again.

See-saw, Margery Daw

See-saw, Margery Daw,
Jacky shall have a new master;
Jacky shall have but a penny a day,
Because he can't work any faster.

Pease Porridge Hot

Pease porridge hot,
Pease porridge cold,
Pease porridge in the pot
Nine days old.

Some like it hot,
Some like it cold,
Some like it in the pot
Nine days old.

Pease por-ridge hot,   Pease por-ridge cold,

Pease por-ridge in the pot   Nine days old.

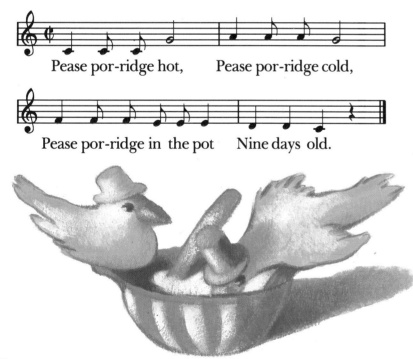

Ring-a-Ring o' Roses

Ring-a-ring o' roses,
A pocket full of posies,
  A-tishoo! A-tishoo!
We all fall down.

Ring - a - ring   o'   ro - ses,   A

pock - et   full   of   po - sies,   A -

ti - shoo!   A - ti - shoo!   We

all   fall   down.

Here We Go Round the Mulberry Bush

Here we go round the mulberry bush,
The mulberry bush, the mulberry bush;
Here we go round the mulberry bush
On a cold and frosty morning.

This is the way we wash our hands,
We wash our hands, we wash our hands;
This is the way we wash our hands
On a cold and frosty morning.

This is the way we dry our hands,
We dry our hands, we dry our hands;
This is the way we dry our hands
On a cold and frosty morning.

This is the way we clap our hands
We clap our hands, we clap our hands;
This is the way we clap our hands
On a cold and frosty morning.

This is the way we warm our hands,
We warm our hands, we warm our hands;
This is the way we warm our hands
On a cold and frosty morning.

Here we go round the mul-ber-ry bush, The
mul-ber-ry bush, the mul-ber-ry bush;
Here we go round the mul-ber-ry bush On a
cold and fros-ty morn-ing.

London Bridge

Lon - don Bridge is fall - ing down,

Fall - ing down, fall - ing down,

Lon - don Bridge is fall - ing down,

My fair la - dy.

London Bridge is falling down,
  Falling down, falling down,
London Bridge is falling down,
  My fair lady.

Build it up with wood and clay,
  Wood and clay, wood and clay,
Build it up with wood and clay,
  My fair lady.

Wood and clay will wash away,
  Wash away, wash away,
Wood and clay will wash away,
  My fair lady.

Build it up with bricks and mortar, (etc.)
Bricks and mortar will not stay, (etc.)
Build it up with iron and steel, (etc.)
Iron and steel will bend and bow, (etc.)
Build it up with silver and gold, (etc.)
Silver and gold will be stolen away, (etc.)
Set a man to watch all night, (etc.)
Suppose the man should fall asleep, (etc.)
Give him a pipe to smoke all night, (etc.)

Oranges and Lemons

Oranges and lemons,
Say the bells of St. Clement's.

You owe me five farthings,
Say the bells of St. Martin's.

When will you pay me?
Say the bells of Old Bailey.

When I grow rich,
Say the bells of Shoreditch.

When will that be?
Say the bells of Stepney.

I'm sure I don't know,
Says the great bell at Bow.

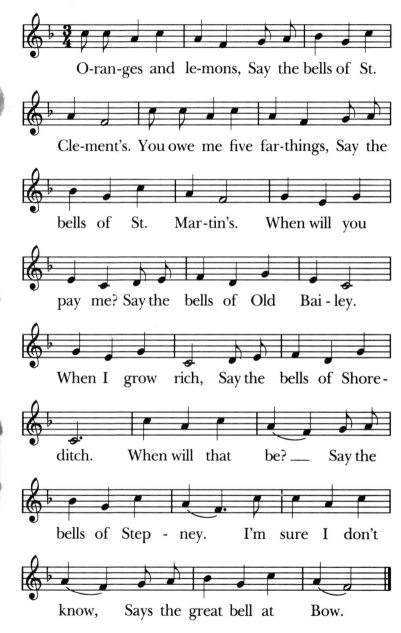

O-ran-ges and le-mons, Say the bells of St.

Cle-ment's. You owe me five far-things, Say the

bells of St. Mar-tin's. When will you

pay me? Say the bells of Old Bai - ley.

When I grow rich, Say the bells of Shore-

ditch. When will that be? ___ Say the

bells of Step - ney. I'm sure I don't

know, Says the great bell at Bow.

Twinkle, Twinkle, Little Star

Twinkle, twinkle, little star,
How I wonder what you are!
Up above the world so high,
Like a diamond in the sky.
Twinkle, twinkle, little star,
How I wonder what you are!

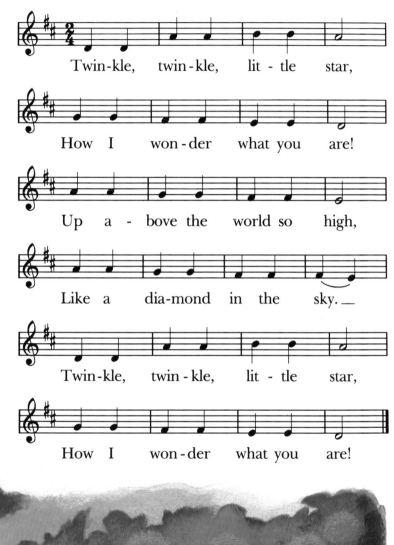

Twin-kle, twin-kle, lit-tle star,

How I won-der what you are!

Up a-bove the world so high,

Like a dia-mond in the sky. —

Twin-kle, twin-kle, lit-tle star,

How I won-der what you are!

Higglety, Pigglety, Pop!

Higglety, Pigglety, Pop!

Higglety, pigglety, pop!
The dog has eaten the mop;
    The pig's in a hurry,
    The cat's in a flurry,
Higglety, pigglety, pop!

Hig-gle-ty, pig-gle-ty, pop! The

dog has eat-en the mop; The

pig's in a hur-ry, The cat's in a flur-ry,

Hig-gle-ty, pig-gle-ty, pop!

Hey Diddle Diddle

Hey diddle diddle,

The cat and the fiddle,

The cow jumped over the moon;

The little dog laughed

To see such sport,

And the dish ran away with the spoon.

Humpty Dumpty

Humpty Dumpty sat on a wall,

Humpty Dumpty had a great fall.

All the king's horses,

And all the king's men,

Couldn't put Humpty together again.

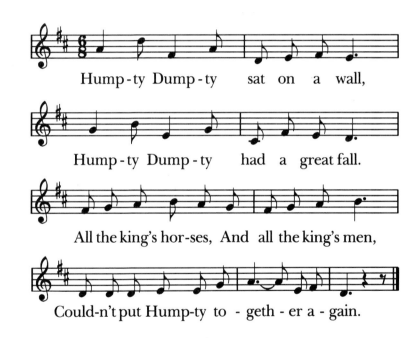

There Was a Lady Loved a Swine

There was a lady loved a swine,
    Honey, quoth she,
Pig-hog wilt thou be mine?
    Hunc, quoth he.

I'll build thee a silver sty,
    Honey, quoth she,
And in it thou shalt lie.
    Hunc, quoth he.

Pinned with a silver pin,
    Honey, quoth she,
That thou may go out and in.
    Hunc, quoth he.

Wilt thou have me now,
    Honey? quoth she.
Speak or my heart will break.
    Hunc, quoth he.

There Was a Man Lived in the Moon

There Was a Man Lived in the Moon

There was a man lived in the moon,
  lived in the moon, lived in the moon,
There was a man lived in the moon,
And his name was Aiken Drum.

Chorus
  And he played upon a ladle, a ladle, a ladle,
  And he played upon a ladle,
  And his name was Aiken Drum.

And his hat was made of good cream cheese,
  good cream cheese, good cream cheese,
And his hat was made of good cream cheese,
And his name was Aiken Drum.

Chorus

And his coat was made of good roast beef, (etc.)
And his buttons were made of penny loaves, (etc.)
His waistcoat was made of crust of pies, (etc.)
His breeches were made of haggis bags, (etc.)

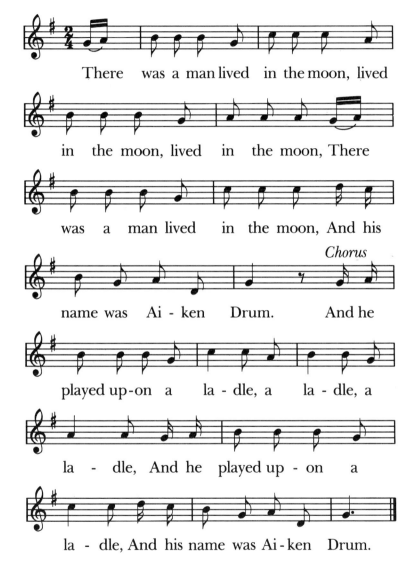

When Good King Arthur Ruled This Land

When good King Arthur ruled this land,
    He was a goodly king;
He stole three pecks of barley-meal
    To make a bag pudding.

A bag pudding the king did make,
    And stuffed it well with plums;
And in it put great lumps of fat,
    As big as my two thumbs.

The king and queen did eat thereof,
    And noblemen beside;
And what they could not eat that night,
    The queen next morning fried.

When good King Ar - thur ruled this land, He
was a good-ly king; He stole three pecks of
bar-ley-meal To make a bag pud-ding.

Hot Cross Buns!

Hot cross buns!
Hot cross buns!
One a penny, two a penny,
Hot cross buns!
If your daughters do not like them
Give them to your sons;
One a penny, two a penny,
Hot cross buns!

I Had a Little Nut Tree

I had a little nut tree,
   Nothing would it bear
But a silver nutmeg
   And a golden pear;

The King of Spain's daughter
   Came to visit me,
And all for the sake
   Of my little nut tree.

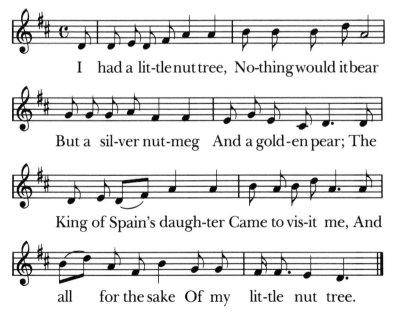

I had a lit-tle nut tree, No-thing would it bear

But a sil-ver nut-meg And a gold-en pear; The

King of Spain's daugh-ter Came to vis-it me, And

all for the sake Of my lit-tle nut tree.

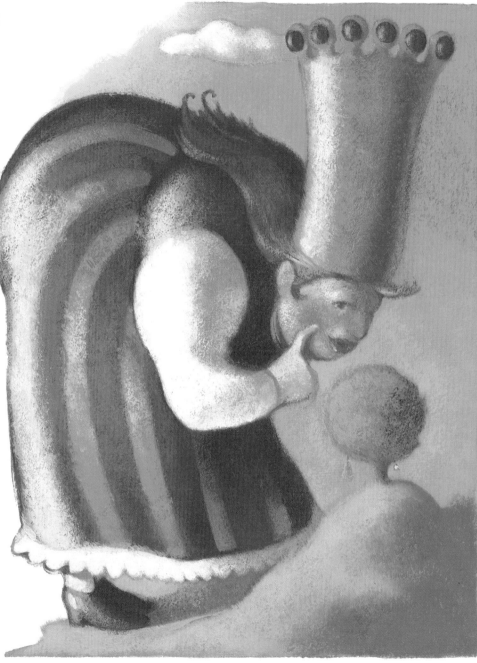

Old King Cole

Old King Cole
Was a merry old soul,
And a merry old soul was he;
He called for his pipe,
And he called for his bowl,
And he called for his fiddlers three.

Every fiddler, he had a fiddle,
And a very fine fiddle had he;
Tweedle dee, tweedle dee, went the fiddlers three.
Oh, there's none so rare
As can compare
With King Cole and his fiddlers three.

Old King Cole Was a mer-ry old
soul, And a mer-ry old soul was he;
He called for his pipe, And he called for his bowl,
And he called for his fid - dlers three.
Ev - ry fid - dler, he had a fid-dle,
And a ve - ry fine fid - dle had he; Twee-dle
dee, twee-dle dee, went the fid - dlers three.
Oh there's none so rare As can com - pare
With King Cole and his fid - dlers three.

I Saw Three Ships

I saw three ships come sailing by,
 Come sailing by, come sailing by,
I saw three ships come sailing by,
 On New Year's day in the morning.

And what do you think was in them then,
 Was in them then, was in them then?
And what do you think was in them then,
 On New Year's day in the morning?

Three pretty girls were in them then,
 Were in them then, were in them then,
Three pretty girls were in them then,
 On New Year's day in the morning.

One could whistle, and one could sing,
 And one could play on the violin;
Such joy there was at my wedding,
 On New Year's day in the morning.

I saw three ships come sail-ing by,
Come sail-ing by, come sail-ing by, I
saw three ships come sail-ing by, On
New Year's day in the morn-ing.

Simple Simon

Simple Simon met a pieman,
    Going to the fair;
Says Simple Simon to the pieman,
    Let me taste your ware.

Says the pieman to Simple Simon,
    Show me first your penny;
Says Simple Simon to the pieman,
    Indeed I have not any.

Simple Simon went a-fishing,
    For to catch a whale;
All the water he had got
    Was in his mother's pail.

Simple Simon went to look
    If plums grew on a thistle;
He pricked his finger very much,
    Which made poor Simon whistle.

Sim - ple Si - mon met a pie - man,

Go-ing to the fair; Says Sim - ple Si-mon

to the pie-man, Let me taste your ware.

Sing a Song of Sixpence

Sing a song of sixpence,
  A pocket full of rye;
Four and twenty blackbirds
  Baked in a pie.
When the pie was opened,
  The birds began to sing;
Was not that a dainty dish
  To set before the king?

The king was in his counting house,
  Counting out his money;
The queen was in the parlor,
  Eating bread and honey.
The maid was in the garden,
  Hanging out the clothes,
There came a little blackbird,
  And snapped off her nose.

Sing a song of six-pence, A pock-et full of rye;

Four and twen-ty black-birds   Baked in a pie.

When the   pie   was   o - pened, The

birds be-gan to sing;   Was not that a

dain-ty dish To   set be-fore the king?

There Was a Crooked Man

There was a crooked man, and he walked a crooked mile,
He found a crooked sixpence against a crooked stile;
He bought a crooked cat, which caught a crooked mouse,
And they all lived together in a little crooked house.

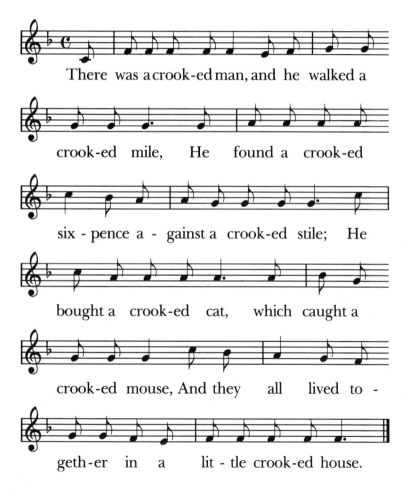

There was a crook-ed man, and he walked a

crook-ed mile, He found a crook-ed

six - pence a - gainst a crook-ed stile; He

bought a crook-ed cat, which caught a

crook-ed mouse, And they all lived to -

geth-er in a lit - tle crook-ed house.

There Was an Old Woman Tossed Up in a Basket

There was an old woman tossed up in a basket,
Seventeen times as high as the moon;
Where she was going I couldn't but ask it,
For in her hand she carried a broom.
Old woman, old woman, old woman, quoth I,
Where are you going to up so high?
To brush the cobwebs off the sky!
May I go with you? Aye, by and by.

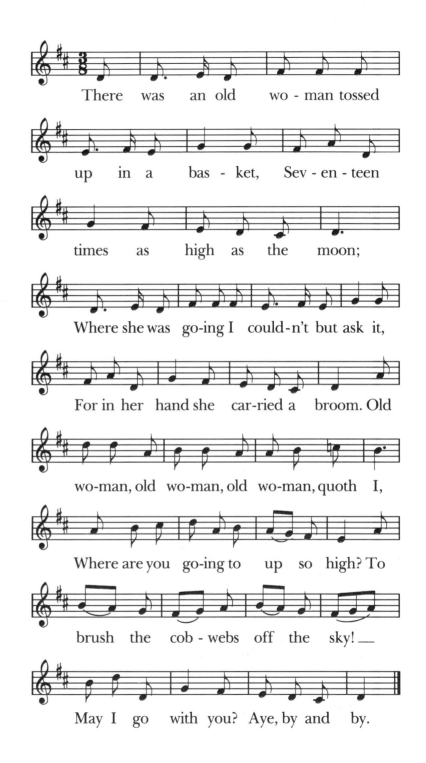

Yankee Doodle

Yankee Doodle came to town,
    A-riding on a pony;
He stuck a feather in his cap
    And called it macaroni.

Yankee Doodle keep it up,
    Yankee doodle dandy;
Mind the music and the step,
    And with the girls be handy.

Curly Locks, Curly Locks

Curly Locks, Curly Locks

Curly locks, Curly locks,
  Wilt thou be mine?
Thou shalt not wash dishes
  Nor yet feed the swine,
But sit on a cushion
  And sew a fine seam,
And feed upon strawberries,
  Sugar and cream.

Cur - ly locks, Cur - ly locks, Wilt thou be

mine? Thou shalt not wash dish - es Nor

yet feed the swine, But sit on a cush-ion And

sew a fine seam, And feed up - on

straw - ber - ries, Su - gar and cream.

Bobby Shafto

Bobby Shafto's gone to sea,
　Silver buckles at his knee;
He'll come back and marry me,
　Bonny Bobby Shafto!

Bobby Shafto's fat and fair,
　Combing down his yellow hair;
He's my love for evermore,
　Bonny Bobby Shafto!

Bob - by Shaf - to's gone to sea,

Sil - ver buck - les at his knee;

He'll come back and mar - ry me, —

Bon - ny Bob - by Shaf - to.

Oh Dear, What Can the Matter Be?

Oh dear, what can the matter be?
Dear, dear, what can the matter be?
Oh dear, what can the matter be?
Johnny's so long at the fair.

He promised he'd buy me a fairing should please me,
And then for a kiss, oh! he vowed he would tease me,
He promised he'd bring me a bunch of blue ribbons
To tie up my bonny brown hair.

And it's oh dear, what can the matter be?
Dear, dear, what can the matter be?
Oh dear, what can the matter be?
Johnny's so long at the fair.

He promised to buy me a pair of sleeve buttons,
A pair of new garters that cost him but two pence,
He promised he'd bring me a bunch of blue ribbons
To tie up my bonny brown hair.

And it's oh dear, what can the matter be?
Dear, dear, what can the matter be?
Oh dear, what can the matter be?
Johnny's so long at the fair.

Oh dear, what can the mat-ter be?

Dear, dear, what can the mat-ter be?

Oh dear, what can the mat-ter be?

Fine

John-ny's so long at the fair. ___

He prom-ised he'd buy me a

fair-ing should please me, And then for a kiss,

oh! he vowed he would tease me, He prom-ised

he'd bring me a bunch of blue rib-bons To

Da Capo al Fine

tie up my bon-ny brown hair. ___ And it's

Lavender's Blue

Lavender's blue, diddle, diddle,
  Lavender's green;
When I am king, diddle, diddle,
  You shall be queen.

Call up your men, diddle, diddle,
  Set them to work,
Some to the plough, diddle, diddle,
  Some to the cart.

Some to make hay, diddle, diddle,
  Some to cut corn,
Whilst you and I, diddle, diddle,
  Keep ourselves warm.

Lav - en - der's   blue, did -dle, did -dle,

Lav - en - der's   green;

When I   am   king, did -dle, did -dle,

You   shall   be   queen.

Where Are You Going to, My Pretty Maid?

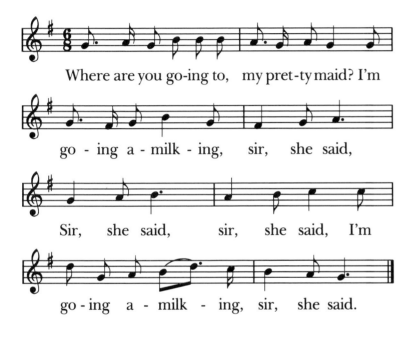

Where are you go-ing to, my pret-ty maid? I'm

go - ing a - milk - ing, sir, she said,

Sir, she said, sir, she said, I'm

go - ing a - milk - ing, sir, she said.

Where are you going to, my pretty maid?
I'm going a-milking, sir, she said,
Sir, she said, sir, she said,
I'm going a-milking, sir, she said.

May I go with you, my pretty maid?
You're kindly welcome, sir, she said,
Sir, she said, sir, she said,
You're kindly welcome, sir, she said.

Say, will you marry, me, my pretty maid?
Yes, if you please, kind sir, she said,
Sir, she said, sir, she said,
Yes, if you please, kind sir, she said.

What is your fortune, my pretty maid?
My face is my fortune, sir, she said,
Sir, she said, sir, she said,
My face is my fortune, sir, she said.

Then I can't marry you, my pretty maid.
Nobody asked you, sir, she said,
Sir, she said, sir, she said,
Nobody asked you, sir, she said.

Dance to Your Daddy

Dance to Your Daddy

Dance to your daddy,
My little babby,
Dance to your daddy, my little lamb;
You shall have a fishy
In a little dishy,
You shall have a fishy when the boat comes in!

Dance to your dad-dy, My lit-tle bab-by,

Dance to your dad-dy, My lit - tle lamb;

You shall have a fish-y In a lit-tle dish-y,

You shall have a fish-y when the boat comes in!

Pat-a-Cake, Pat-a-Cake

Pat-a-cake, pat-a-cake, baker's man,

Bake me a cake as fast as you can;

Pat it and prick it, and mark it with B,

Put it in the oven for baby and me.

For baby and me, for baby and me,

And there will be plenty for baby and me.

Pat - a - cake, pat - a - cake,   ba - ker's man,

Bake me a   cake   as   fast as you can;

Pat it and prick it, and   mark it with B,   Put

it   in the o - ven for   ba - by and me.   For

ba - by and me,   for   ba - by and me, And

there will be plen - ty for   ba - by and me.

Hush-a-bye, Baby

Hush-a-bye, baby, on the tree top,
When the wind blows the cradle will rock;
When the bough breaks the cradle will fall,.
Down will come baby, cradle, and all.

Hush-a-bye, ba - by,   on   the tree-top,

When the wind blows the   cra - dle will rock;

When the bough breaks the   cra - dle will fall,

Down will come ba - by,   cra - dle, and all.

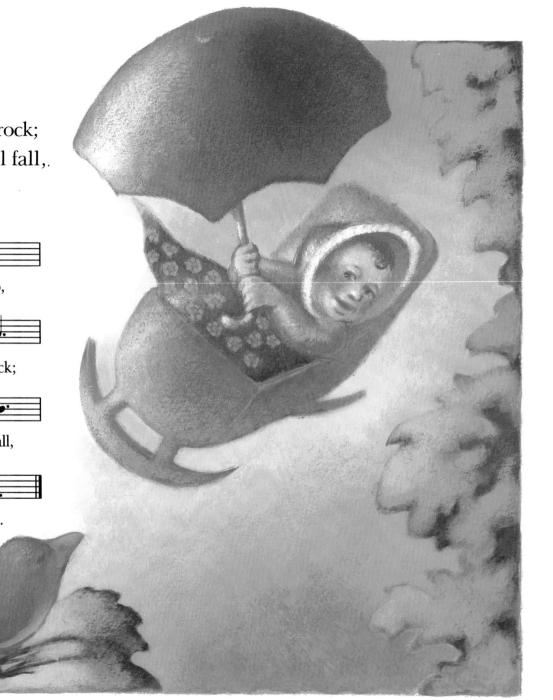

More About Mother Goose
Notes About Selected Nursery Rhymes
Index of First Lines

More About Mother Goose

Many of these nursery rhymes date back to the beginning of the seventeenth century. Most were the creation of individuals whose identities have been lost, or perhaps of small groups, adding and editing as they sang together. Through the years these songs have been handed down by word of mouth, with variations in wording and melody creeping in. So the song your neighbor sings to her children may be somewhat different from the one your grandmother taught you. Both may vary from the popular versions in England or Scotland. But that is the way of oral literature!

But what about Mother Goose? Was there a real Mother Goose? Scholars have debated this question for years. The name "Mother Goose" came into the English language through the translation of a little book of fairy tales published in France in 1696–97. The author was a French scholar, Charles Perrault; the title: *Histoires ou Contes du Temps Passé avec des Moralités (Histories or Tales of Past Times with Morals)*. Facing the title page in that book is a picture of an old woman spinning by the hearth. Overhead is a plaque that says: "Contes de Ma Mère

l'Oye." Literally translated, this reads: "Stories of My Mother the Goose."

Perrault's book contained eight stories, including "Cinderella," "Little Red Riding-Hood," "The Sleeping Beauty" and "Puss in Boots," but no verses or songs. In 1729 these stories were translated and published in England as *The Tales of Mother Goose*—still with no verses or songs.

The success of this book led to publication of another English volume, *Mother Goose's Melody; or, Sonnets for the Cradle* (c. 1765). This was made up of fifty-one "songs and lullabies of the old British nurses," plus sixteen lullabies from William Shakespeare.

American printers of the eighteenth century, who were quick to pick up successful books from English publishers and print them with little change and no permission, brought out an American edition of *Mother Goose's Melody* some years later.

Although we think of the Mother Goose rhymes as being for young children, only a few seem to have been created for that age. These include the lullabies, baby-play songs, and counting-out rhymes. Some of the other rhymes made their debuts as songs in stage productions for adults. Others came from plays performed by mummers, who went from house to house to entertain on festive occasions. Many are old ballads or folk songs that children seem to have adopted as their own. Several were political campaign songs. A few are the cries of street vendors.

Through the years there have been repeated efforts to identify various Mother Goose characters with political figures of the time. For example, it has been suggested that "Little Boy Blue" represented Cardinal Woolsey, and that it was Queen Elizabeth I who rode the "cock-horse to Banbury Cross." (Or was it Lady Godiva?) Iona and Peter Opie, the scholarly authors of *The Oxford Dictionary of Nursery Rhymes*, state: "...the bulk of these speculations are worthless."

Until the eighteenth century, few of the old rhymes were recorded in print. Some of the first printed collections of the rhymes used the word "song" or "melody" in the title but included no musical notation. Were they songs in the literal sense? We don't know for sure. We do know that the melodies have survived for a goodly number of nursery rhymes and that new melodies—and other rhymes—are created from time to time.

The simple melodies used in *Songs from Mother Goose* have been adapted from several nineteenth-century songbooks long out of print.

The old melodies, like the old words and verses, have the wonderful lilt of oral literature—singing, swinging, repeating, and singing again. These rhymes invite participation with words that rhyme and echo. Further, they lend themselves to dramatic singing—deep voices and piping voices, husky voices and gentle voices, pigs grunting, roosters crowing, pussy cats purring.

Most important, they give children the chance to take part—by singing the pretty maid's answers to the questions in "Where Are You Going to, My Pretty Maid?" Or echoing the repeated phrases in "London Bridge." Or acting out the Old King Cole drama as it is being sung. Or creating new phrases and lines for such a song as "Aiken Drum."

Notes About Selected Nursery Rhymes

Baa, Baa, Black Sheep

This is one of the rhymes included in the earliest known book of nursery rhymes, *Tommy Thumb's Pretty Song Book*, published in England (c. 1744). The melody is also that of "Twinkle, Twinkle, Little Star."

Bobby Shafto

During the British election of 1761, this song was widely used by supporters of Robert Shafto, a candidate for Parliament.

Boys and Girls Come Out to Play

The words and tune of this nursery rhyme date back to the early eighteenth century, when it appeared in dance books with directions for the dance and in *Little Pretty Pocketbook*, published by John Newbery (1744). Later it became a neighborhood summons for children to "come out to play" in the evening.

Dance to Your Daddy

The words and rhythm of this well-known Scottish nursery rhyme suggest dancing the baby or toddler on your knees as the song is being sung.

Here We Go Round the Mulberry Bush

This singing game is believed to go back to the eighteenth century. Children sing as they go round and round in a circle. Then, as the words direct, they stop to go through the motions of washing their hands, then drying, clapping, and so on. Children love to add new stanzas and thus prolong the fun.

Hey Diddle Diddle

This is probably the most popular nonsense rhyme in the English language. It was included in *Mother Goose's Melody* (c. 1765). In the late 1880's Randolph Caldecott created an enchanting picture-book version of this nursery rhyme that sold for just one shilling.

Hickory, Dickory, Dock

This is believed to have been a counting-out rhyme, which children used to determine the leader.

Higglety, Pigglety, Pop!

Samuel Griswold Goodrich, the American author of the Peter Parley informational books for children, ridiculed the nursery rhyme as worthless. "Any child could write one," he said, and proceeded to make this one up in 1846.

One hundred twenty years later, the famous American artist Maurice Sendak wrote and illustrated a book for children entitled *Higglety, Pigglety, Pop!* In his book, the star is Jennie, Sendak's Sealyham terrier, who eats a mop (made of salami) each day and twice on Saturday.

Hot Cross Buns!

Years ago the city of London was often a bedlam of street cries from itinerant hawkers loaded down with such wares as milk, mousetraps, old clothes, brooms, feather dusters, pies and cakes, footstools, and sausages. Each vendor had a special cry or singsong chant for his or her wares. "Hot cross buns! One a penny, two a penny, hot cross buns!" advertised the buns marked with a cross and sold on Good Friday morning. From the noisy streets of old London, this street cry has become a favorite nursery rhyme.

How Many Miles to Babylon?

Children who played this old English singing game altered the first line to name their own town: "How many miles to Wimbledon?" for example, or "How many miles to Coventry?" Early American printers easily made the change to "How many miles to Boston town?"

Humpty Dumpty

This popular nursery rhyme is probably one of the best-known riddles in all literature. Children love the discovery that Humpty Dumpty is an egg. And they relish Tenniel's illustration of Humpty Dumpty sitting on a garden wall in *Through the Looking-Glass* by Lewis Carroll.

Jack and Jill

Through the years this old rhyme has been extended to fifteen verses and has been the basis for innumerable pantomime and puppet shows as well as spontaneous drama at home and at school.

Lavender's Blue

The traditional seventeenth-century words and tune of this song have made it a popular rhyme in the nursery. In later years it became a dance tune for adults.

Little Jack Horner

Since the early eighteenth century there have been tales, histories, and printed music about Jack

Horner. One legend has it that Jack Horner was a messenger instructed to deliver a pie to the Abbot of Glastonbury. He is said to have opened the pie on the way and found valuable documents inside, which he promptly appropriated. Whether true or not, the nursery rhyme makes a splendid base for pantomime and improvised drama.

Little Miss Muffet

Many scholars have tried to determine who Miss Muffet really was, but the question that children ask is "What is a tuffet?" There is no convincing identification of Miss Muffet as a real person, but we do know that a tuffet is a stool.

London Bridge

Because I grew up in an area where we sang, "London Bridge is falling down," I find it hard to accept "broken down" as a frequent alternative in both ancient and modern books of nursery rhymes. Whether broken down or falling down, the bridge presents a mystery, for it seemed to vanquish every builder.

As a game, London Bridge has entertained generations of singing children, who line up to pass under a bridge formed by two players, each grasping the uplifted hands of a facing partner. When the "bridge" falls down, the child who is caught goes out. The game and song in countless versions are part of the oral literature of many European nations as well as England and the United States.

Mary Had a Little Lamb

These four-line verses, among the best known in the English language, were written by Mrs. Sarah Josepha Hale of Boston and first published in 1830. Later they were included in *McGuffey's Second Reader* (1857) and have been popular ever since. Although several people claimed to be the original Mary of this little song, Mrs. Hale refuted their claims.

Mary, Mary, Quite Contrary

For at least two hundred years scholars have been trying to determine whether this rhyme was directed to Mary, Queen of Scots. Were "the pretty maids all in a row" her maids-in-waiting? Nobody knows, but the guessing goes on.

Oh Dear, What Can the Matter Be?

This romantic folk song dating back to the eighteenth century has become a nursery favorite— in part, I suspect, because of the chorus. Children love to adapt the chorus to fit an immediate situation in their lives. And many a parent has spun out a parody of the first stanza to bring comfort to a child in tears.

Oh Where, Oh Where Has My Little Dog Gone?

Although created as a drinking song by an American, Septimus Winner, this has become a favorite for the nursery here and in England.

Oranges and Lemons

Almost any visitor to London brings back memories of the chiming of church bells, each with a different tune and apparently a different song. And in many old songs the bells of various London churches sing out their messages. "Kettles and pans/Say the bells of St. Ann's" and "Brickbats and rifles/Say the bells of St. Giles" are among dozens of variations.

Pat-a-Cake, Pat-a-Cake

Even the word "pat-a-cake" seems to suggest the simple clapping that delights a toddler. You can add a little drama by patting out the "cake," then marking it, and baking it "for baby and me." For older children, this song makes a good hand-warming exercise on a cold day.

Pease Porridge Hot

This can be a wonderful clapping game for facing partners. Each claps his or her hands; then partners clap their two rights, then each to his own, then the two lefts. On and on the variations go, faster and faster until one partner gives up.

Polly Put the Kettle On

Even this simple old rhyme takes on a bit of drama when sung as though calling an unresponsive Polly in the next room—at first in gentle tones, then a little louder, finally in a commanding tone.

Ring-a-Ring o' Roses

Here we have the song for a popular game for little children who join hands to form a circle, go round and round as they sing, then give two lovely sneezes, and "all fall down."

See-saw, Margery Daw

Children playing on the see-saw enjoy this old song. At one time it may have been the work song of men using a two-handled saw.

Six Little Mice Sat Down to Spin

In Beatrix Potter's tale *The Tailor of Gloucester*, the little mice sing this song, which was already well known as a nursery rhyme.

There Was a Man Lived in the Moon

Repeated lines within each stanza and the swinging chorus make this old Scottish folk song popular with today's children. American youngsters delight in substituting some of their favorite foods for the less familiar delicacies mentioned in the song. Don't be surprised if they sing, "And his coat was made of pizza pie, of pizza pie, of pizza pie" and "His buttons were made of bubble gum, of bubble gum, of bubble gum."

Three Blind Mice

This song is particularly amusing when sung as a round.

Tom, Tom, the Piper's Son

Don't let children worry about the fate of the pig. Probably it was not a live pig, but a sweetmeat shaped like a pig and sold by a street vendor. It might have been made of a sweet pastry stuffed with currants and baked.

Twinkle, Twinkle, Little Star

With the title "The Star," this little poem by Jane Taylor first appeared in 1806 in *Rhymes for the Nursery* by Jane Taylor and her sister Ann Taylor. It has become one of the best-known poems in the English-speaking world. The melody is that of an old French tune, "Ah, vous dirai-je, Maman," which is also the basic melody of "Baa, Baa, Black Sheep."

Where Are You Going to, My Pretty Maid?

This is a wonderful song for question-and-answer chanting or for pantomime.

Yankee Doodle

Although "Yankee Doodle" originated in America before the American Revolution, it was taken over by British soldiers as a song of ridicule of the backwoodsmen of New England. But as the British met defeat at the hands of these same Yankee Doodles, the song became the pride of the American forces. It is said that they played it triumphantly as they marched to accept the formal surrender of the British at Yorktown. By now "Yankee Doodle" has become one of the most popular songs of both English and American children.

Index of First Lines